REQUIEM FOR INN(

By

Alan Chester

Published by
The National Poetry Foundation
27 Mill Road
Fareham
Hants PO16 0TH
0329 822218

Typeset by:
Intereurope Technical Services Ltd.
Fareham (0329) 822420

Printed by:
Meon Valley Printers
Bishop's Waltham (0489) 895460

To Mary Maher, who gave me so much initial help and has contin-
ued to do so.

Sponsored by Rosemary Arthur

C.V. Photo courtesy of Farmer's Weekly magazine.

Cover drawing by Anne Christie.

Previously published in Orbis, Otter, Staple, Pause and Farmer's
Weekly and featured on BBC Radio.

ISBN 1 870556 85 2

£3.90

CONTENTS

Alan Chesterfield. A product of generations of Cornish extraction who emigrated to Plymouth and later as far as Exeter where I was born far too long ago. Married to a doctor , with two sons, one a dairy farmer the other a solicitor. Qualified in medicine from the London Hospital, applied for overseas service with the Royal Navy and served my time in the Royal Army Medical Corps in Kent! Practiced for twenty five years, mainly general practice in Birmingham, then, sixteen years ago, retired to take up farming and have graduated to a dairy herd of eighty cows, a few sheep and bullocks on about a hundred and fifty acres in North Devon. Did a bit of writing (prose) and won odds and ends from competitions, in very small pools, before venturing in the ocean of poetry, where there have been a few landfalls, many voyages and numberless shipwrecks. I am very fond of the countryside and its people, enjoy humour and dislike war and intolerance, all very run of the mill stuff, and all of which influence my work, but I do try not to preach!
I have received great help and encouragement from two circles of poets, both established and budding, in North Devon who listen and praise (rarely) or criticise (often), but always constructively, and would thoroughly recommend such a course to any closet poet. I have received continuous encouragement from The National Poetry Foundation and Johnathon Clifford, who must regard any bouquets for this book as his, the brickbats are mine alone to cherish.

SCENTS OF SMELL.

You remember younger days?
Do you recall time...and beauty?
The scent of lilies,
The silence of forget-me-nots?

I remember baking days.
Fresh crusted bread, cakes on the rack,
The pungent nip of jam on autumn fires,
Or, warm before the Christmas blaze,
Savouring those December smells
Of Patum toast, of cheese and celery
On tables mirrored by beeswax.

I remember blackboard smells.
Chalk dust laced with teacher's feet,
And round the back the antiseptic bogs
Tobacco smoke with lysol on its breath.
Then every day was summer of light airs,
The murmuring of bees, and honeysuckle scent
long fields of corn and poppies.

I remember days of heavy airs
When every hour was winter in the soul.
Do you recall the smell of death,
The smell of fear, of fear of death,
Of fear of dying slowly -,
The scents of lilies,
The silence of forget-me-nots?

"Remember me." The swirls of mist
The gelly smell of heat, of floods and spots.
Perfumes of Leichner five and nine,
Adrenaline and dust.
Regal, in mists of tulle and spirit gum,
The ghost of Hamlet's father breathes
Murder and pickles and brown ale.

I remember Columbines;
Women shadowed by time.
Wraithes of hair and face and form
Who have no name, comforting;
Warm invited beds offering
Love or lust or sanctuary
To Harlequin, in loneliness.

1

I recall cathedral halls of trees.
Dib-dob, wood-smoke smell of sanctuary.
Incense memories of canvas wet with dew
Where meadow sweetened wind on tensioned guys
Hummed requiems for innocence.
Odours of sanctity and drum-role rolls
Of honour by the emptied pews.

Oh! I remember all these things
That fade with time
To leave the scent of lilies,
The silence of forget-me-nots.

WRITERS' COURSE.

Some come for love of words;
The music, rhythms, rise and fall
Of stress and scansion on the page,
Soft spondee footfalls and the anapest
Enmeshed, entrapped in timeless lines.

Some come in search of power,
Command obedience in the written word,
Mark hope or fear or prejudice,
Seek truth or beauty, weigh the cost
Of paper and the death of trees.

Some come to play a sly roulette.
Secrets, hopes and childhood dreads; echoes
Too private still to pass the tongue.
Truths that would offend the listener
Who reads the code with no Rosetta stone.

CANDLE LIGHT.

much kinder than the neon tube,
smoothes etching time from tested faces.
Candles glow on fireside tables.
Linen frosts and silver traces
crystal sparkling cold as virtue
reflect the funeral pyres of bees.

Of course, comb-honeyed wax is best,
outbidding humble paraffin,
it filters fear and, shading time,
feeds fantasy where scented flames
perfume the funeral pyres of bees.

Of course, it fuels the fires of faith;
illuminates the path to God
reflects the resurrection theme and
torches truth from children's eyes
beneath the funeral pyres of bees.

Pride can't afford to see beyond
the ruby at the finger's end
or cost, in pain, the furs that wrap
the vanity of little men
chilled by the winds of cold disdain
that fan the funeral pyre of bees.

The measured world's a stage.
Eyes barn-door closed
The back drop presses and
Hope takes wings and flies.
In long, day-longing night
Limes are a bitter fruit
Where black gel is the fear.
Pick up the tab.

Flat flat worlds. Set
A fingertip proscenium arch
Defines the apron.
The snake-eyed die is cast.
Leichner is grease.
Paint without purpose
By touch and smell
Prompts each-day dreams
Halcyon, golden coloured
Time that runs for ever.

The groundling cheers grow faint.
The Columbine in widow weeds.
Harlequin shrouded. Clowns
Costumed in darkness.
Bring down the curtain.

LOCK OUT OUTLOOK.

There is no need to lock the toilet door.
There's no one to disturb me.
I sit and think, of times when there would be

Morning bathroom queues, and toast and corn flakes
The scamper off to school. Then, I would
Swallow tea and, running, grab the toast
Pray butter would not drip to mark my sleeve and
Will the eight fifteen to be as late as yesterday.

Now, as the day awakes
I lie and hear the trains go by.
I swallow tea, and nibble buttered toast.
I do not pray.
It does not matter if the butter drips.
There is no need to lock the toilet door.

I quite refuse to dye my beard, or
implant hair upon my head or walk
with sticks that emphasise my age. I
use such dodges as I may, and hear
the passers-by remark, "He is a
wonder for his age," as I stride past.

I march along the Mall or through the park
with head erect and shoulders braced, until
my breath gets out of step, and then I stop
to smell the flowers, inspect the plumber's store
or, leaning at the boutique window, pant
at articles of feminine attire.
"It is a wonder, at his age," they wink,
"The D.O.M. You'd think he would be past
that sort of thing." It's memory that gives
the game away. I write myself a note
to list two things, start walking to the shops
then pause, sniff pansies in a window box
or pat the dog and pass the time of day.
-Oh God what is this wretched woman's name?-
"Hello, my dear," I say, "Now, isn't this
-What is her husband's name?- a pleasant day.
I hope that -er- is feeling well." In shops
assistants chat and, polishing their nails,
remark, "It is no wonder. It's his age,"
as they ignore me while I stand and wait
and ponder where I put the note.

THIS WAS NOT THE PERSON THAT I KNEW.

I will not miss the thing that died today.
This was not the person that I knew.
A skeleton that lay on rubber sheets, wrapped
loosely like a parcel with that weary skin
where suffering was written by the lines.
I did not know the eyes that skulked, in sockets
punched like crutch prints in the snow, dead eyes
that danced those few short months ago.
Where is the mouth that kissed and laughed at life
that, drawn by pain across the too large teeth,
grins in a rictus of contempt for friends who grieve?
This was not the person that I knew, who vibrant
as a child, plucked wild music from the air,
who sang delight composed from harmonies of youth
when gentle hands soothed fear, stroked lullabies
and wiped away the tears. Whose claws are these?
Whose talon fingers searched, to counterpoint
the rattle of hard breath with silent fugues
plucked, chin high, from laundered sheets?
This was not the person that I knew, when
hand to hand we passed along mapped ways until,
beneath the probing and the microscope,
our roads divided at the X-Ray sign. Then,
as I watched, you smoothed away from me, to fade
and reappear and fade in mists of pain, re-present
the present timeless time with flashes of the past.
I will not recognise this thing that was my life, and
I will close my mind, refuse to give a name.
This was not the person that I knew.

LATE NIGHT LONDON LAUNDROMAT.

By night the winter window frosts, garish
in neon frenzy, condenses steam that trickles tears
to pools of urgent colour on tired paint.
On plastic chairs grey spectres hunch, half turned
against acknowledgment. Hedged in by silence
they dream of sun kissed ecstasty and dead eyed
watch the absolution suds, behind the glass,
swirl confidential spoil from lonely worlds
of Yale lock doors and crusted lino stairs.
Night walkers, they cache the day light dream
against dark hours of desperation. Shadowed, they
fold the stainless penance wash in plastic bags
then, armour-wrap themselves with plastic macs
and dread to leave ephemeral friends
who do not raise their eyes to see them go.

OLD PEOPLE'S HOME.

Un-sexed, they sit in fireside chairs,
pastel and slippered in grey limbo lands; lone
worlds of the frozen frame, blanket wrapped
against the draught of years that
cancelled friends against the unpaid debt
of loneliness. Shadows, they fence themselves
behind blank walls of silence and sleep
to bar the way to conversation, for they
have said it all before and
who is there to listen?

BOG MAN SACRIFICED.

Strangled by cord. Leather
By peace and peat, replacing skin
You lay immortal, unnatured
In two thousand years.

As the cord tightened did you believe,
Did you believe your God would save you?
Did you think your soul, in passing
Would bring the harvest
Or did you not believe in gods
Yet paid for grace by proxy?

We find your solitary death obscene.
Contemptuous, condemn as pagan
Ritual, murder. Our Gods of Love
Count sacrifice in thousands;
Perfumed, incensers harvest servitude
to chants and absolution to a candle's light.

BUS-PASS BIRTHDAY.

and I am lonely in my mind.

They swirl around me, cry
'Surprise,' stoop, kiss my cheek
and wish me well, rain presents on me
stand to drink my health.
We joke and reminisce, spatchcock
my aspirations with my years, laughing
remember who and when and where. Quiet
we grieve for absent, ever present friends

and I am lonely in my mind.

Embraced by love, they hedge me in,
press too close to savour friendships
garnered over time

and I am lonely in my mind.

FAMILY CIRCLE.

Soft as kitten paws
Hands holding time
Clasp my finger
Explore yesterdays.

So small, they cup
The world, and knead
The milked half-globe
Of their universe.

My immortality
Twice removed. I
See me in eyes
Of blue amazement.

A tiny enormity
Grasps tomorrow
In hands so small
They cannot ring my finger.

CHRISTMAS TIMES.

Before the journey to the midnight mass
we gift-wrapped dreams in crepe. On tiptoe,
crept down creaking tell-tale stairs
to heap on heap the secret parcels
underneath the tree. Wide-eyed, we peeped
at labels, then resolved to greet the book
with valour and a spurious delight, to
face the absence of that special bike
in private desperation.

Through debris studded years of tinsel
crepe, and carols sung beneath the fairy wand,
we passed from bikes to Pop and girls and
wine beneath the tree. Then we would plunge
the iron into the ale and turkey trot,
pour brilliant, brandy words to waste
in unreceptive ears and writhe beneath the spell
of mistletoe to steal the parasitic kiss, and
lie and dream forgotten dreams until
the fire's light died.

In shadowed passing of the years
the ashes of those days of nights grew cold.
Now, quickened by the woodsmoke pall compressing time,
and comforted by awe in children's eyes, the
diuturnal embers glow and age transmutes
ephemeral joys to happiness.

WOODSMOKE AT CHRISTMAS.

In axe sharp days we blow upon our nails,
collect the wood that crackles in the hearth
to scent the air with apple wood
and pine and yesterdays' regrets.
In baubled swathes we dress the tree
then gift-wrap hope before we kill
the sacrificial lamb, applaud the hunt
preserving deer, stoop, to collect
sad broken pheasants bred for fun.
Sated, we sing. Commemorate compassion
beneath red-berried wreathes of holly.
To candle incense, light the fairy world
in glory, see ourselves reflected
in eyes too young to understand.

PAINTING DAYS NUMBERED.

In burning burnt-sienna days
I sat and painted skeletons of trees
that stretched beyond the flesh of leaves
to prick the clouds. Soft petal drop, ripe fruits,
the cradle-rock of falling leaves, gold rain
to sprinkle fallow fields; the autumn days
of brown-spot spatter on the backs of hands,
when outlined talon-bones begin to show.

In muted greyed-tone colour days
I paint the fingered skeletons of trees,
hands pleading for the sky, etched dark
against the light; blue-shadow drifts and snow
on grounds where green-spike snowdrops grow.
Snow bearded, winter frosts my winter bones,
dead fingers wake beneath the see-through skin,
when green-shoot grandsons reach to take my hand.

PAS DE DEUX.

Look back, to read
our choreography of days
written, ebb and flow,
by edge of seas. At springs
foot prints converge, mark
on the sands footloose
reverse perspective and
pirouettes that meld to step
by step into the parallel.
Scalloped, two fringes trace
uncertain childhood tracks
deepen, cast adrift, beach
beyond horizons on shores
where other feet inscribe
to different tempi and
to unfamiliar airs.
At neap the footsteps slow,
weave patterns of pavanes and
disappear at turn of tide
where rolling time sweeps in
to leave no mark, no memory
that we had joined the dance.

WINTER IN TOWN.

I breathe winds of spice and caraway
cross dolphined seas in white sail ships

-White sails? Yes, white I think
against the blue-

                  white, full belly sails
trimmed. Alive, with fine tuned mast
and burgee flying with the stars. Anchor.
Naked dive, trail silent diamonds, fly
with angels, drift to sands of powdered pearl

-That's nice 'Powdered pearl's nice-

sands powdered pearl. Palm-shaded, snooze
where sun bakes colour out, drink nectar
from long frosted glass. In evening sup
ambrosia with friends. Night breathes
winds of spice and care away dream moonshine
girls in Lotus lands

"One tea. One cod and chips
One thirty, dear."

Bliss lives
in lands of twisted metaphor.

SAM. SON AND DELIGHT? AH!

Sam's Dad was In The City
His mater on the screen
Samuel at Winchester
Rebecca at Roedean.

Sam did not like the City.
"I might become a monk."
"Cool man." Plucked a mean guitar
as 'Educated Punk.'

Beccy thought Mod Rocker Wayne
the best thing since sliced bread.
She studied at the Sorbonne
to graduate in Bed.

Dad's typing temp was pretty.
Mum found a Mexican.
Sam's habits were disgusting.
Pals called him Caliban.

Dad now lives in penury,
Mother in East Cheam.
Samuel's "Friends with Harry,"
Rebecca with Karim.

The shame, and oh, the pity
Things will never be the same
For Samuel's 'in' at Parliament
While Rebecca's on the game.

LOTT'S WIFE.

A beauty queen called Agnes Blott
laid down a lot for what she's got.
She'd friends in every social class
and so, in time, it came to pass

she qualified as fille de joie,
to graduate as the devoir
of half the gentry in Debrett,
and nearly all the foreign set.

She knew delicious little things,
(that constitute the sports of kings,)
and loosened pockets of the boys
who gave her most expensive toys

like gold and jewels and oil wells.
They even offered wedding bells.
Fair Agnes, keeping to the rails
collecting sordid little tales,

shook many an ancestral tree
when sold to tabloids for a fee;
sent shivers through the House of Lords.
(And tawdry bawds the Lords affords.)

At last she wed Augustus Lott
(so quickly got the lot he'd got,)
retired, pro temp, and took a cruise
and read of Spiro in the news.

Spiro, the second one she led
to the multinuptial bed,
made Croesus look as if deprived
and then conveniently, died.

Divorcing husbands three and four
collected oil wells near Lahore.
Wed number five - a year last week -
"My dear, another ancient Greek.

He may have had his Cretan chips
but left a dozen fleets of ships."
Her Arab husband, number six,
proved oil and water do not mix;

so, at the present going rate,
she'll soon be owning half Kuwait.
She's living here with vast estates
behind enormous wrought iron gates,

staff (burnoused) there wait upon her
(slyly called, 'Her guard of honour.')
Now, as she counts her double chins
and wages of a life of sins,

she opens functions by the score
and visits hostels for the poor.
Revered by all, she's seen to be
a pillar of society.

BULRUSHES.

Moss Bros's. sister Marilyn
under the influence of gin
fell whilst washing Moss' laundry
at the stream where all and sundry
washed dirty linen, laundered sin,
and gossiped about Marilyn.

For Marilyn was quite a girl
prepared to give it all a whirl,
would lead the boys a merry dance
until the day she met, by chance,
a tall and eager handsome churl
who said, "I'll wed this priceless pearl."

His vestal pearl? There was a catch
to imperfect the perfect match
Alas, alack, and here's the rub,
she found she'd joined the pudding club.
She thought, I've hit a purple patch
A little plot I'll have to hatch.

So, with tears and maiden's blushes,
told a tale about bulrushes
begged the quack, a confirmed cynic,
"Send me where that special clinic
operates, and also hushes
up results of Panic crushes."

So Marilyn and churl were wed.
Besotted, on the wedding bed,
he wept to hear the whispered plea
"Please, gently dear. Be kind to me,"
like many blushing brides have said
with fingers crossed and virtue fled.

NO, HONESTLY, I AM GIVING UP!

Stolen from Sir Walter Raleigh.
(and serve him right)

Conceit begotten by the eyes
Is quickly born and slowly dies,
For while it seeks our hearts to have
Meanwhile sweet reason makes his grave;
So many things the eyes approve
Which yet the heart doth seldom love.

For as the seeds in spring time sown
Lie in the earth until full grown,
Such is the weed whose rooting kills
In heart and lungs and maketh ills
It makes of ever freeman slave
And drags him breathless to his grave.

Affliction follows fortune's wheels
And soon he's shaken to his heels,
Thus sealed, by coughing, is his fate
And liking still is turned to hate.
Whilst all afflictions have their change
Foul cancer only loves to range.

Desire himself runs out of breath
And smoking doth but gain in death.
Longing nor reason hath not rest
And blind doth seldom choose the best.
Habit attained is not desire
But as the cinders to the fire.

But yet some poets fain would prove
Tobacco is the perfect love
And that the weed is of that kind
A mild disorder of the mind.
Praise God that I, before I'm hearsed,
Shall hear the name of Raleigh cursed.

(Anybody got a fag?)

23

HOLIDAY BREAK DANCE.
(A walk from Lumb Bank to Hebden bridge and back)

Cut loose to stride, hop-skip and glide
above green valleys greyed in golden heat.
History mourns on silenced mills
where ivy weeps, where hump-black walls
stitch quilts of patch worked fields
and buttercups shroud hills veiled in mist.
Now, step down shadowed steps, where mosses grow
on granite treads sculpted by time. Birds sing
in foxgloved woods, and fern-frond skirts
dress trees cramponned to slopes above the stream.
Set silent foot-falls on a thousand years
along cool-dapple paths soft to the bones of leaves.

March to Eve's Mount.
Box house ranks parade, black on red
sentry-go, beneath grey walls of sycamore
blued in a tarmacadammed haze.
To martial beat of drums and pipes - on tape -
'By the right, quick march,' through Raleigh Way
where furnace roads vibrate and
slow tar tears explore the gutter's edge.

Slow march
through rose-red Eve's View's tiers, stacked
red-rose, regimented beds and lawns cropped
'Back'n Sides.' The Woman broods in black.
Delphic, on watch in Western Avenue, sits
dead-eyed knits purple in unrelenting sun.
Her thumb points downhill to the right.
"Straight down, turn left for Hebden Bridge."

DOWN THE HILL.

Outside the school below the road, litter bins lean
spill spoil of coke and crisps and chocolate
childhood paradise. 'Please Shut Me,' pleads the gate
that swings on empty playgrounds beside the church
where hours are golden in blue time. Grave stones
black with memory and age, speak of Hebden's Bridge of old;
days before we numbered wars, speak of, 'William Hartley
Beloved Son,' secure behind iron railings, and
remember 'Helen,' who never saw a Spring. A fly
blows immortality on a sparrow fallen between angels.
From the tower St. George's Cross, white as sepulchres,
whips and crackles against grey thunder clouds.

BACK TO TEA TIME.

Re-cross the water-garden stream
peopled by ducks and blossom Cola cans.
Pass timeless Counties tapping time; timeless
rhythms old as time. Clock-watching, sweepers
curse the day, and crest the never ending hill
where virtue marches nine strait miles; and
no right turns to Heptonstal, beyond the pale.
On time, at four the Micro Rider leaves,
past stones where time is past and Helen sleeps.
Cascading kids whoosh down the street, whoop-greet
and swinge and sing on swinging gates.
The Woman's rapiers purl to tea time pips, and I
review Eve's view of Raleigh Way; breathless
remount Eve's Mount and climb long woodshade ways.

Lumb Bank bakes and mashes tea; then waters
zeugmas, hope, and footsteps spring.
Oh, cakes and four o'clock belong to me
in fragrant hours when birds and kettles sing.

The passages in italics are from Kipling's Jungle Book

Wood and Water, Wind and Tree
Jungle favour go with thee.

JUNGLE BOOK.

Fat black ash by the altarstone.
Here is the white foot rain.

Skeletons of trees, decay,
Tooth-stub trunks
Half-buried, bleached
Among marram tufts.

Now turn the page.

Man goes to man.
To the Man-trail
We may not follow.

Hard wood bones, fingers
Stripped of flesh, signpost
Dead villages
On tarmacadam routes. Point,
Where food bowls
Corrode on mosaic
River beds, now.

Turn the page.

The pools are shrunk
The streams are dry
And we be playmates, Thou and I
'Til yonder cloud

Hot red dust
Spirals, red
Hot thermals
To dead seas.

Turn the page

The promise of Tha
Is the Promise of Tha.

Now jetsam, scaffold halls
Of whales, beached
By progress,
Echo to rhythms tapped
On muffled drums,
When time marched
Out of step. Now

Turn the page.

And these were my companions.
Pity 'tis they died.

Prop-up elephants
Carved in ivory,
Cut out rhinoseri
Ground to lust
Roam, in lands
That glow at dark,
Drink, where rains
Turn litmus red.

STALAG 77 AUTUMN.

The sun is yellow, backlighting wire
Necklaced with dew.
The wire is an endless boundary
Bounded by a rolling breath of mist.

The fields are furrowed, highlighting wire.
Garlanded barbs.
The wire is a faded memory
Hidden in a Joseph's coat of leaves.

The year is timeless, spotlighting wire
Eaten with rust.
The wire is tensioned periphery
Softened to a galaxy of jewels.

REQUIESCAT FOR SHADES
On hearing Britten's War Requiem

From battle they, the shades, pass back.
Mists in mist. Poets unversed, saints
sinners and the simple man, all reapers
reaped, fallen, silent
beneath the purging of the guns.
Shadowed from life, they grin and
trip the geiger count, endless
march in noiseless lines. At reveille,
to laments and broken trumpet calls,
they melt above their bones and
lines of crosses painted white.

WALL OF RESISTANCE.
(St. Saturnin)

'Fusilles contre ce mur.'

It was the wall that brought it home.

Plain. Stones
Laid end to end.
The future ended
Here, against this wall
Near fifty years ago.

Armel Collet.
Jean Fossier.
Paulette Nourean.
Robert Lebely.
Four names engraved.

A hamlet
That would not fill a disco hall.

'Fusilles contre ce mur.'

It was this wall that brought it home: that
And the fresh picked flowers that trembled in its shade.

EXMOOR CROSSROADS.
(Day)

Today, I sit on timeless rock
By Blackpits Gate by Hoar Oak Tree,
To watch the sun flare in the east,
Ignite the amethystine ling
And torch the drip-drop bracken fronds.
Sun-warmed, web spangled fields emerge,
Stretch where the diamond-studded sea
Curves up to opalescent sky.

Wash on pastel wash of colours
Flush the impasto moor from skies
Where buzzards quarter, needle eyed
And silvered, ice-high, vapour trails
Scrawl wistful, sun-kissed hieroglyphs
Of dreams in light, of worlds beyond.
Curlew call and birdsong anthems
Herald the nascent dew-fresh day.

In black on light at Kinsford Gate,
The tussock ewes watch dancing lambs
In moorland ballet pirouette,
Break candyfloss, enchanted webs
That fairyland the spears of reeds.
Afloat in mist, dressed black on white
Milk-heavy, cudding, patient cows
Come home to berth by Combesland Cross.

Framed in sweat and sunbeam haloes
Four Exmoor ponies amble up,
Inspect me, shrug, then saunter on
To melt as soft as memory.
There, in the corner of the roots,
A form of hinds reviews the dawn,
Surrounds the stern school-master stag
That poses on a nearby knoll.

There; from the Cleve a flash of red.
There; braying horns, the huntsman's cry.
There; baying hounds stream down the hill:
There; lines of watchers, scenting blood.
They, with bright expectant faces
Relish the sun, commend the day
Banter and laugh and all agree
This is a perfect time; to kill.

Mocking, this Exmoor smiles by day
Soothes haunting fears that darkness brings,
Yet flaunts what crawls beneath the stone
When the skylark sings.

She was doormouse small to me
even when I was a child.
Now she is no bigger than a dried leaf,
where bone shows brittle without flesh
as if she would crumble at a sigh.
She sits in fireside chairs and
in the absent grate sees
fields and moors and
dreaming home, smells woodsmoke
baking and the warmth of byres, feels
velvet flanks of cows against her cheek
and udder-warms her hand, or mittens them
beneath the down of hens to pilfer eggs.
Lost, she calls lost sheep and daily
hopes to hear the shepherd's call
to take her in.

AUTUMN MILK.

Hit the alarm and curse the day
that's only half awake. Humph
out of bed across uneven boards,
raise the blind and slow-eyed
watch the sun review the earth
bury its head in clouds
to sleep again.

Stump 'up along.'
Swear patient cows from fields
to parlour, here at home. In groups of four
they stand and eat and steam. Warm milk dances
into vacuum jars to metronomic tick-clock
tock-clicking rhythms of machines.
Sucked to iced-cold stainless tanks it cools
and waits for Scottish Oats or Shredded Wheat
in Shepherds Bush or Cheam.

KETTLE BOILING.

Today he did not dip his bread
in brackish morning tea, or throw
the breakfast scraps to hens that crake
beside his door. He shrugged the pain
to milk his cows and turn them out.

At home his kettle, simmering on the range
breathes steam that cools, to dribble from
limed walls and pool on flags, or mist on nails
burnished by his shoulder sacks. Content
his cat sleeps in his chair.

Sun-rise above the parlour
polishes the coats of cows. Spectators,
they cud and stand in circles, or tiptoe
past the dog that howls.

DEAD STOCK.

He must have been a little man.
I found his first-war boot today
behind the wood-store stable
where empty hay racks
stand higher than my head. Hob mail
it marched in war, hobnailed
trudged with blinkered Shires
in narrow furrowed peace.

Shire's shoes hang on beams
above the kitchen range. Settled
I sense his presence here, and
at the gate resting, thoughtful
chin on hand, to smoke or
sucking straw, comparing costs
of barley corn his gran'fer's father tilled.

I found a first war boot today
and half a gaiter too small
to go around my wrist.

DAIRYMAN.

Sleep dragged to day leaves clawmarks
scored behind long lids on eyes that shun
the frosted window hiding snow whispered
by night to lie cill deep. Drowned asleep
despatch a toe to scent the icy room.
Pupate to long johns and long-tailed shirt
warmed beneath the quilt, and woollen socks.
Don corduroys and chatter into sweaters
one, two, three. Noble in stealth creep
down the edge of stairs too soft to wake
the sleepers still adrift in seas
of unberthed dreams.

Cringe to iced boots, breathe liquifaction
thaw thick parlour frost then waken cows
who do not welcome me. They stand and stamp
curse at the clusters dreaming sleep, grumble
back to stalls to cud the broken night away.
Now wash the parlour, sterilize the line
inspect milk warming in the minus zero tank.
O.K. Run home.

In blizzard dawn stamp
out of boots and unsuccessful mac
to shiver in the kitchen's Aga warmth.
Revel in piping tea with new day milk, thick
butter soaking golden toast with marmalade
that never saw a grocer's shelf. Deal with
the post fill another bloody census form
ring A.I. ring the vet do the VAT order cake
fill another bloody census form, and chase
the man who promises the part, again. Before
the daily chores take up the breakfast tray
to guests in bed, who wake and wonder
what you find to do all day.

LIMBO LANDS.

The words in italics are the names of parts of the plough. The hinge of the tractor door I use as a sight along a furrow, so that the furrows are parallel when marking out a new section of land to be ploughed. These are called 'Lands.'

Diesel the tractor. Check the oil.
Hitch the plough. Inspect its parts.
Beneath encrusted walls of grease
Crossbeams and *Shares* and *Skims* and *Shins*
And *Draft* are names that my forefathers share,
But *Top-link* that belongs to me. Ease in
High on the seat and carry on
In borrowed tractor half as old as mine.
Through doomsday, horse day, muddied lanes
Of fern and hazel, alder, thorn and eglantine.

Now to the brown-green stubble fields.
The rubble, stubble, trouble fields:
Level the plough and draw the headland line
And sight the hinge that marks the lands.
From Oak Tree, write the silver staves in light
That point and vanish at the rising sun.
In heartland turn, inscribe the treble clefs
Against the headland at the river's edge.
Furrows curl and whispering sighs
Cocoon the mind with lullabies.

Now. Watch the hinge that marks the lands.
To tittle tattle battle lands.
Get out the shades against the sun.
Swig mugs of brackish tea. And curse.
Eat sandwiches or buns or cake. And curse
And broil in the midday sun. Bompety bom
Bompety bom. "Order the oil. Order the feed."
'I will," said Bill. "Settle the bill.
Order the straw." "I will," said Bill.
But he hasn't. Unreliable sod forgot.
Forgot the spare *Share*. Order *Share*
Spare. Spear. Pears. Pares.
Reaps. Rapes. Apers. Apers?
Parse. Parse all understanding.
Order. Order.

So. Watch the hinge that marks the lands.
Dream tit and rattle battered lands
Of milk white tors, of endless thighs.
Bompety bom, bompety bom, bompety bom.
Wendy and Pam and Leslie Thing
Old thingy's sister. What's her name?
Tester or Pester or Lester. Oh! Lester
Less lie, less stir. Ho. Ho. Hot.
Mop the brow and wriggle in the seat.
Top link? To plink. I plink. Thou plinkest.
He plinks. Quick. Check the line. The line
That spills into the willow hedge. All right.
It's a furrow, furrow better thing that I

Ho. Watch the hinge that marks the lands.
Lands short. Short lands beyond the edge.
Taken short. Hop behind the hedge. Stand
And chat to pheasants eating corn. Wave
To shaken ramblers - who believe in nature.
The *Share's* O.K.? Fair shares? O.K.?
Burton's up and I.C.I. I spy with my T.I.
Something beginning with Shell. Shell's up.
Shell stars. Star-shell. Star shells
Shelled in hubble-bubbled, rubbled fields
of finger claws and furrowed thighs,
And children's faces full of eyes

That watch the hinge that marks the lands,
The ever Never-Never lands. Ease the aching
Back. Bompety bom. Can't feel my bum. *Draft?*
Feel the draught. Draft ox. Box and Cox.
Wet lands. Drift. Adrift. *Crossbeam?*
Cross-bills. Fly away birds. Cross
Bills. Break the sod. Break the sterile pan.
Fly Peter. Fly Wendy. Fly to dream mountains
Limned in gold against the setting sun
And bare branch trees of roosting rooks

And watch the hinge that marks the lands,
The loaming, gloaming, homing lands.
Head aches. Heart aches. Headlands. Headlines.
Head lines. Brow furrows. Bompety bom
Ho bloody Ho. *Hoe-plough.* Home. Plough.
Home. Twilighted home to milk the cows,
and milk-white hills, and broad leaved woods
Coppiced by love in measured time,
To watch the hinge that marks the lands.

MORNING MIST.

In Jack Frost night earth's breath condenses,
snuggles foot-muffed hills in fleecing mist
and early dawn: beyond the toast rack and
the steam of tea, the picture window frames
new worlds of lost perspective - backlit treetop
islands, homeless rooves and cattle drift
in silent seas - heliotrope by sunrise. Probing
against the sky, the steeple waits for light
to purge the golden vane above the grave
stoned body of the church. Cows paddle, belly deep,
above the clouds, where Scoter heads of sheep bob
and dive in mist to fish for cobs.

As day awakes I watch the sun undress the fields.
Spinneys emerge on banks of streams where iced shards
chatter over stones, in sunlight cold as diamonds.
To tocsins and the ring of bells the rag rook
rumbles into flight, and bare-rib branches shiver
obligatos on to frozen ponds. Icicles
along the picture edge drop sunlit worlds
from needle tips.

Because he could not write or read They
smirked behind his back and said that
William was an ignorant man.

For sixty years he lambed his ewes
and sheared his sheep. He told his problems
to his cows who nuzzled him and did not mock
because he could not write his name. The pen
was not at home in thickened hands
that fondled wood, to fashion beauty with an adze
or whittle poetry with a pocket knife.
"Poor old boy," They said, behind Their Hands
and shook Their Heads and sighed.

He did not feel the need of books,
for William heard the Word at church,
and spoke with birds. He read the clouds
and knew by heart the stories in the dew.
He could decode the message of the months
published in muddied foot-print runs
by friends and foes from fields and would
relate their secrets to their times and
tell the curving paths of lives and deaths.

He married Meg before the war. Childless
he called her 'Mother,' until the day he died.
Today They read his will. They said that the
aforementioned William hereinafter the testator
gave devised and bequeathed his hereditaments
goods and chattels in toto without let or hindrance
to his spouse with the proviso that she did not
predecease him or fail to survive for thirty days
from his demise in which event—

After fifty years, he had little to leave her
but his love. They knew *Omnia Vincit Amor*
was a Latin tag, but William was a simple man.
He did not know of Virgil. He could not even read
or write his name, but he had known the truth of love
yet, They had thought Old William was
the ignorant one!

TEA AT WEST COMBSLAND.

Tea on spotless lawn where friends meet
over bread thin as an excuse,
jelly of blackcurrent flesh, purple
on yellow crusted cream and butter
which is different. Cakes
light as thistledown on floral plates
that came when Mother died.
In floral cups, tea coiling fragrant
steam awakens fragrant memories;
those sun filled days. Lucullus dined
on Sunday afternoons at four.

There's salmon paste for Sue who
"Can't take cucumber now, " and
fruit cake for Sid who's "Partial."
Moist pyramids of coconut
which I love, 'happen'
by thoughtfulness.

Hay's finished... Her's pregnant...
He's working in a mission hospital.
Corn's looking good... It's her fourth...
So Eileen's cousin said...
Cows doing?... It's a shame, poor soul...
Mind you, he always was a bit
'that way'... Mmm... Ah... Fair.
After the last time... He broke
his mother's heart... Ah... She's
never been the same since... But
he went, any way... Mmmm.

Talk of no importance flows
of little vital things that wash away
the dross, and leave the seedcorn nurtured
by a simple meal fashioned by caring.
Cream in Mother's cut glass dish and
remnant cakes, bagged, to take back home
to remember.

LOCH SIDE BY NIGHT.

Below the trees that coat the sweep of hills
the waters, still as fear, menace,
hold back the clock, hiding their depths
in black, reflecting heaven. In peace
they promise peace where cones of pines
fall upwards to the clouds, beckon
where tiptoe mountains wade in quiet
deep as thought.

From loch side reeds a curlew calls
a piping, lost soul, *pibroch* cry
that silences the silent siren-song.
The fish-rise on the mountain peak
re-swings the pendulum, splinters the moon
down polished paths, to treacle-slide
in river pools and on, like troubled time
through waterfalls of tumbled stars
to bleach on waves and probe the fringe
that underlines the certainty of seas.

SHEEP DOG PASSING.

He said, "You needn't wait
if you'd rather," and called the nurse.
"It's for the best," He said.

Whose best I'd like to know. It's
all very well for Him
all glass and stainless steel.
"It will be very quick," He said,
and filled the syringe.
"There will be, no pain." He said
and clipped the hair above the vein.

Holding her, she licked my hand and
understood; anything would be a piece of cake
after nights of blizzards on the moors
to pinpoint buried sheep, and rescue lambs
or, to a whistle, in the noontide heat
outrun, collect and fetch far flocks
from hills to lusher lowland grounds.
Her eyes reminded me of little things, shared
times to treasure garnered over half a life.

"It's done," He said
and dropped the needle in the stainless bowl.
At peace she watched me, sighed and slept.

Him, his glass and stainless world
said there would be no pain:
but He was wrong.

They've finished the Link Road to Heaven
and Exmoor is open at last.
The Gateway to pastoral Devon
is 'Three lanes' and , 'Ever so fast.'

There's forests of slender lamp standards
instructions, 'Give way to the right'
there's directions to Taunton
and beaches at Saunton
in floodlights of floodlights of light.

There are islands of white painted bollards
there's festoons of telephone wires
electricity pylons
that go on for miles 'n
the tourists in pig styes and byres.

Now the numbers of roads are all different,
"Us can't be expected to know
t'other from which 'n
with Twitchen spelt Twitchan
God knows where the grockels will go."

Oh! there are plans for building car racetracks
and similar countryside joys.
They're reviewing enactments
and building embankments
to comply with statutes on noise.

Where the influx of tourists expected
to listen to blackbirds and larks
they'll hear songs of the robin
and residents sobbin'
in acres of landscaped car-parks.

There are bridges that run upon rollers
and viaducts terribly tall;
what with lay-bys and cuttings
where stags did their ruttings
there's no bloody Exmoor at all.

VILLAGE CHURCH.

I distrust those gods that need incense, vestments and
the panoply of pomp; false heavens where acolytes
parade, mine profits from the depths of fear, mount guard
where sacred treasure rests in vaults and then
on high in pulpits preach the worth of poverty.

Guarded by elms
the village church tap-roots
where heartsease and blue speedwell blow
amongst grave time-worn stones.

At home in soil,
millenium bones are laid
that prayed and paid in tithes
for near a thousand years.

On vellum books
of rusted ink and watered silk
our quarter-vicar registers torn time,
our history colour-fast; today
in Biro black.

Like jewels
in Norman niches of thick granite walls, small
treasured vases of a wildflower spring
reflect on lists of springtime names -
graved, polished, timeless,
brass memorials
to stolen lives of war.

Cool in the calm the silence speaks
the small voice in the inner private ear.
His is the quiet little chat
borne on the scent of new mown hay.

I rose at five and killed you.
Blacklead birds, nailed
to doors of coops where unborn,
chicken lie, in shattered worlds
like broken promises.
Your eyes unsee the red-eyed hate
that blinds to beauty, slow
black mood magic of your flight.
I weep for butchered children
torn mother care, and feel no guilt
to pin you to the door or
hang the bodies on the fence; and yet
I wonder where the line divides,
separates your guilt from ours. You
only know survival's need, yet we
in wisdom disembowel the world,
with vision watch it bleed,
anaesthetise compassion, unfeeling
spurn the pangs that pin us
to cathedral doors of consience.

COUNTY SHOW.

You can sort the farmers from the other folk. Red faced,
they stand around the Guinness tent and gently sweat,
clutch tankards to their chests with weathered hands
and lean on shepherds' crooks to talk, (a lot!), of sheep
and quotas and the shocking price of feed. In the ring
they strut - important - parade the polished beasts
before a judge who knew it all - until today-,

*"Bugger's blind. That, best in show? N'couldn't
beat a three legged rigg!"*

(but there's always one to recognise his skill.)
Work done, they drift through lanes of subtle siren-song,
the syrup dealer smiles that promise bargains, booze and
rest for aching feet.
In tents, that sport designer barrels and unlikely grapes,
New Barbour Coats above Green Hunter Boots sip wine and
think that country living must be fun, with nothing much to do
but lie in feather beds

"It must be true, Old Boy. I heard it in the House."

and take the Missis' Rolls to Town

to bank another grant.

"Old Boy, I know a chap who read it in the press."

The Fountain-head of jam, Jerusalem and News spills wives
to curse their husbands at the Guinness stand, who
nestle tankards to their chests and — contemplate.
They sit and sweat, smile beatific smiles,
and do not talk a lot.

SILENCE.

"It is too quiet," he said,
As we walked by the river.

Town man, sit with me.

Let us listen to the music
Of silence.
Hush. Can you hear the air
Sigh
In the heat
Hum
In the alders?
A will o' the wisp
of sound.
An aeolian harp
Sleeping.

Listen to the plash of rising fish,
Grace notes in the chorus
Of the evening birds.
See? See where the water vole
Explores the pool, spearheads
glissandoes that necklace the stream
in diamonds.

Do you see the kingfisher dive?
There. There, to catch the rainbow fish
In multicolour counterpoint.
Do you hear the drums?
Why, the kettle drumming of the rabbit
Seeking sanctuary.
Put your ear to the ground.
Hear the earth breathing?

Still.
Hear the slither of slow worms
In dry grass,
The patter of the mouse
Through nettles,
The twig's stroke,
Sounds of trees
Talking.

PROVENÇAL MARKET.
(L'Isle sur la Sorgue)

Earth colours, washed in sun
to constant tone of sandstoned light,
streets in shadow-shades of lavender
and scent of herbs from Mayfly stalls.
Fruits of land and labour vie
where flowers frame the flyboy and the artisan.
There on a stall of artists' dreams
a doubtful book supports a Daumier sketch.
White muslins curve in Mistral's wake;
cobweb parabolas, where great walls
reflect and splinter in the Sorgue.

Different from home,
the granite and grey rain. Small
nests of stalls of eggs and honeyed combs,
produce from farms; the cattle, sheep
and lambs that pass to greener fields.
But people interchange, the Provençal
who prods the Devon fare with Gallic thumbs
while Devon fingers poke, and point
and ask the price of artichokes
in universal tongue of eyebrows raised.